HOW T
KEEP YOUR WIFE
in Love with You
FOREVER

John and Lisa Comandari

Diamond Enterprises
Lakewood, Colorado

ISBN 0-9666913-1-8

Publisher: Diamond Enterprises, Inc.
2654 South Kline Circle
Lakewood, Colorado 80227

Cover and book design by Jennifer Hancey

HOW TO KEEP YOUR WIFE *in Love with You* FOREVER

This book is designed to make men aware of what women need and expect from their husbands. Many men really try to be good husbands but they never had the support from their family or they lack personal experience to be good husbands. Many marriages fail because they don't know how to do or say those little things to make the other one happy. This may occur because the man does not listen to his wife's needs. Loving your wife isn't enough. Many men love their wives but lack the knowledge to keep the marriage together in a way that sustains the sparks.

This book was written by a married couple to share the secrets from both a male and female point of view. You are going to get all the information that you ever wanted and needed to have a perfect marriage. We have learned tremendously from our families. They have taught us the little secrets that will change your life forever.

By the time you are finished with this book, you will know how to be the best husband any woman could ask for. This book is going to be short and to the point.

We know that when you got married and said I do, you did not receive a manual for making your wife happy and maintaining a good marriage. Even if you had received one, you probably wouldn't have read it anyway. Many men don't read directions very well. (That may be why there are so many VCRs that are not programmed.) We are going to give you all the directions you will ever need to be the perfect husband. All you need to do is read and follow them.

Contents

Acknowledgments

The list continues to grow as we think of all the people to whom we would like to express our appreciation for their support, input, suggestions and hard work in making this book possible.

We thank the Lord for the sacred relationship he has given us. We have been blessed with a wonderful family, great friends, and the power to love one another.

We would like to thank our parents for making two decent human beings, very considerate and very caring about people and about life itself. We also thank them for showing us the right path of a good, honest life and teaching us the importance of good manners. Love was big in our family and always will be. We are all close and love each other very much.

We also would like to thank John's grandparents, may they rest in peace, for all the love they shared and for their commitment to teaching the importance of loving someone with all your heart and appreciating them regardless of the circumstances. They always told us not to take anything for granted.

Special thanks to the rest of our family, Olga, Oscar, Videla, Doug, Steve, Judeh, Sandra, Mark, Michelle, Summer, and the many married couples we interviewed for sharing all those beautiful moments of love and happiness with us. Their insights have made us a closer, loving couple. Thanks for answering all those questions concerning your personal life and for sharing the good and the bad times with us to teach people about being a better husband and friend.

We want to thank Crystal Photo Studios for the beautiful picture on the front cover. Crystal Photo Studios is located in Morrison, Colorado.

Many thanks to Jenny Hancey for designing the book cover and for being so patient with us every time we changed the colors. Thank you for all your hard work.

Last but not least, many thanks to our editor and friend Denise Hmieleski, who worked so hard to get this book finished in time. She did a wonderful job.

Introduction

Common sense, giving, compromising and loving is all you need to have the perfect marriage and the perfect relationship. In addition to our own personal experience, this little book is packed with secrets from our grandparents, parents, and members of our family. They have taught us their secrets and now we will share them with you.

John's grandparents were together for fifty-five years until death parted them. They were the perfect married couple. In our family it was a ritual to go to the park at least once a month for a picnic. I often observed my grandparents holding hands and showing each other how much they were in love. Theirs was a love so powerful it spread anywhere and everywhere.

John's grandfather would often kiss Grandma three times on the cheek to show her how much he loved her. Each kiss symbolized the words "I Love You." When they argued he would make everything better just by giving her those three kisses on the cheek, ending the argument immediately. The power of love and the power of compromise are so wonderful. With those powers you can make someone very happy.

This book will help you become a better husband and everything any woman could hope for in a man. It will show you how just a few simple words or a little gesture can make a difference in your marriage or in any relationship. It's easy and it works. This book will give you the prescription for true love and eternal happiness in your relationship.

LOVE...

is patient and kind;
love is not jealous or rude,
or conceited, or proud, or provoked;
love does not keep record of wrongs;
love is not happy with evil,
but is pleased with the truth.
Love never gives up;
its faith, hope and patience
never fail.

1 Corinthians 13:4--7

Chapter One

The Art of Communication

If you want a love message to be heard, it has got to be sent out.

To keep a lamp burning, we have to keep putting oil in it.

—Mother Teresa

In the first few chapters we are going to walk you through a few of the little things we've learned from many married couples. Through numerous interviews, we gathered a list of needs and complaints from women. The big issue with most couples is "communication" or rather, the lack of communication. All the women we interviewed expressed this, yet many of the husbands we questioned agreed they didn't know what steps to take to fill their woman's needs.

The greatest complaint of married couples is that they just don't talk anymore or they're too busy going in different directions and fail to share things with each other—whether it's discussing daily events or just relating how they feel about each other. Communication is very important. It makes the world go round. You need to tell each other how you feel; what you like and dislike.

How can you communicate better? You need to leave some free time during the day to share and express to one another what problems you may have or things you would like to accomplish in your relationship. True communication, the kind that we are seeking, is the bonding of spirits. Communication can be an interpersonal miracle which allows us to get inside one another's skin, and to know and be known truly by another human being.

Communication is listening and being receptive to the conversation. What we tell one another helps us to know what we think and feel and helps to keep a deep connection with each other. Most of us can talk, but that doesn't mean that anything meaningful has been said or heard. Listening is extremely valuable to the conversation. When listening we need to show we care with our response.

Whether speaking or listening, you can deepen the level of intimacy by openly communicating your feelings, making both of you more aware of what you need to do to make each other happy. Here are some specific points:

Criticize Carefully

When it comes to criticizing, always remember that you must do it in private and never in front of friends. Complaining about small or innocent things, even when done in a joking manner, does nothing to solidify your relationship.

When you criticize in public, it can diminish your dignity and keep you from correcting whatever it is that needs to be improved. It might even bring back some painful childhood experiences. Preserve your love by keeping silent about the things you would like to correct until you are in the privacy of your own home.

In one of our interviews a couple told us that in the past they were guilty of criticizing each other in public. They had developed key phrases especially designed to hurt each other. Once a partner criticized or uttered such a phrase, the name calling would begin and both of them would lose control, blasting each other with every hurtful expression that came to mind.

Tom and Sue were humiliated at a party when Sue noticed Tom looking at another woman more than once. Sue, being jealous by nature, exploded with verbal punishment against Tom. Sue was calling him every name in the book and she brought up other things that he had done in the past, creating a scene that couldn't be stopped with words. It took two police officers to bring them back to reality. Thank God no one got hurt. The situation was out of control and could have ended with violence.

They have since learned that if they have a problem with each other or they want to criticize the other for a mistake or an accident, to do it at home in private and in a civil manner. They learned the hard way how to express their feelings towards each other. They also learned never to use verbal punishment with each other, especially in public.

Apologize

Every time you acknowledge your flaws and you apologize for small or big mistakes, or the things you innocently forget to do, it clears the path to your loved one's heart, which can get blocked with little resentments. Apologizing is a way of keeping current with your relationship and making sure the two of you aren't hurt or holding a grudge for something the other one did or said in the past.

A good apology consists of three essential parts:

- State your crime(s) by name.
- Say you're sorry.
- Ask to be forgiven.

It's really very simple, but so hard to do. When you make a mistake, apologize: "I'm sorry. You're right. I did forget to make the plane reservations. Would you please forgive me? I'm sorry I yelled at you. I'm sorry for not listening very well."

Don't be defensive. Just apologize and everything will work out. When you are defensive you keep the relationship problem going. An apology gives closure to the situation and it opens the road to a new beginning. A genuine apology that comes from the heart is one of the best healers of any problem or situation that you may encounter in your relationship.

Share your dreams

This is very important. Dreams represent some of the most precious parts of yourself, whether they are dreams you have at night or hopes and future goals you have for your lives. Because they are so private, it's understandable for you to create intimacy surrounding them. However, revealing your dreams and goals is an act of trust and even if they don't come true in your lifetime, you will have your loved one to comfort you.

Mark and Angie are another of the couples we interviewed. They shared some of the dreams and goals they had when they were younger. Mark always dreamed of being a police officer and Angie was very supportive. He always shared his dreams and goals with her; dreams of having a good salary, a nice home and cool adult toys like a sports car, boat or motorcycle.

Mark knew he was going to achieve his dreams someday, but he wanted to do so only by being a police officer. He did not want to get a job working anywhere else. He wanted to wait for that special job.

Angie was the only one working at the time. She had to pay all the bills and living expenses. This lasted for about six months and finally she made Mark get a job. It didn't matter to her what kind of a job it was, she just wanted him to do something.

He found a job as a security guard for a few months until he became a police officer. After the first year on the force, Mark started making good money and many of his dreams and goals became a reality.

This is a perfect example of how sharing your dreams and goals with your wife (and working together as a team) will help them become a reality for you.

Always choose loving words

We all want to hear how much and why we're loved; to be reminded why we're special and irreplaceable to the one we love. We want to be singled out and told that we are loved above anyone else. Nothing sustains romance better than love words generously and endlessly spoken.

What we say and what we hear others say has the power to sculpt our experiences, our view of the world, and perhaps most important, our view of ourselves. One of the great gifts of love is the ability to bring life, enlightenment, and healing to the person we most adore.

Words spoken to us by our loved ones truly have the capacity to heal bad memories and old nasty pains. These beautiful words of love have the power to change reality. Therefore, treat those words as healing instruments and as words of magic to bring peace and happiness to your relationship.

As a caring husband, a man converses with his wife in a way that enables her to reveal her deepest feelings. Through conversation you learn to meet many of her needs, but the conversation itself meets one of her most important marital needs — she simply wants you to talk to her.

The four elements of true communication are:

1. **Speaking** or sharing a message to reveal a specific meaning. For example, when you tell your wife that you are having problems, whether it's the way she spends money or problems with intimacy in your sexual relationship, be specific and to the point. Tell her what you need from her and what you need her to do to make it better. Ask for her suggestions for a solution. You might start by saying to her, "Lisa, I've noticed that lately you've been spending a lot of money on clothes and our credit cards are charged to the limit because of this. How can we fix the problem?"

2. **Listening** and being receptive to the meaning of what is being said. Try to genuinely take in what the other person is saying.

3. **Responding** with words to what you have heard and revealing how it has made you feel. You should respond specifically to her questions. Show that you care about the subject she is concerned about. Help her to feel good about the answer you give and always answer with honesty.

4. **Acknowledging** that you have received the response and indicating the way it has affected you.

Only when all four elements, **speaking, listening, responding** and **acknowledging** are present, has a communication taken place. In speaking, we tell who we are and what we feel. In listening, we receive the meaning of what has been said and get a sense of who the other person is. In responding, we show that we have received the message and that we care. In acknowledging the response, we show that we appreciate the other's caring.

Here is a summary of the ways you can care for your spouse through conversation. We've dealt with all of them, now it's time to put them into action.

1. Remember how it was when you were dating. You both still need to show that same intense interest in each other and in what you have to say, especially about your feelings.

2. Your wife has a profound need to engage in conversation about her concerns and interests with someone who cares deeply about her and for her. You need to show her that you really care about her every time you engage in a conversation with her.

3. Get into a habit of spending at least fifteen hours each week alone with your wife, giving her undivided attention. Spend most of that time in a natural but essential conversation.

4. Remember that most women stay in love with men who have set aside time to exchange conversation and affection with them. They stay in love with men who constantly meet their communication needs. Women love to talk and to express their feelings very frequently. They are much more interested in getting to know everything about a person and will ask many questions to feel closer to you.

5. Financial topics should not interfere with your time of conversation. If you don't have time to talk about personal feelings and/or needs in your allotted time alone with your wife, your priorities are not arranged correctly.

6. Never use conversation as a form of punishment (ridicule, name-calling, swearing or sarcasm.) Conversation should be constructive, not destructive.

7. Never use conversation to force your wife to agree with your way of thinking. Respect her feelings and opinions, especially when yours are different.

8. Never use conversation to remind each other of past mistakes. Avoid dwelling on present mistakes as well.

9. Develop an interest in each other's favorite topics of conversation.

10. Learn to balance your conversation. Avoid interrupting each other and try to give each other the same amount of time to talk.

11. Use your conversation time to inform, investigate and understand.

    A caring conversation boosts the marriage tremendously. When you and your wife have a deep conversation, you experience deeper feelings of affection.

Chapter Two

COMPROMISE: A POWERFUL TOOL

Love is not a competitive sport. Winning in love comes through cooperation, compromise and caring. When we become masters of these skills everybody wins.

—Anonymous

Another major thing we learned in our interviews with married couples is that men don't like to compromise. This is a biggie! In order for your relationship to work, you need to learn the fine art of compromise. It's crazy that you always want to be right and always want her to do the things you want, when you want to do them. Women need to have their way too! Going along with her ideas may mean some sacrifice on your part; however, many women have a good imagination and can make things exciting for you.

Men and women usually differ in the type of entertainment they enjoy. For instance, many of the men in our interviews said they prefer watching action movies with a lot of killing and loud sound effects while the women told us they love watching romantic or feel good movies. Women like to relax and watch a movie with a lot of love scenes. They enjoy movies that relate to real life situations or something that has happened to them in their own lives.

Women are more sentimental than men. This goes back to early childhood because women are taught to cry and get their feelings out, whereas men are told, "Don't cry. Be a man." This is probably why men aren't as sentimental as women. Men need to realize that there is more to life than action flicks and lots of scary movies.

As a couple, we have learned to watch more sentimental, feel good movies than action movies. It brings us closer together when we do this. We have learned that when we've had a stressful week at work, an action movie is the last thing we need to watch.

A *feel good* or romantic movie will make you forget about that horrible week you had at work. It helps you appreciate being with your wife at that particular moment and just being alive. You learn to appreciate the little things in life, something we all need to do from time to time. Comedy movies are also great! Everyone needs to laugh a little more in life.

Keeping an open mind with your woman is important. Let her improvise sometimes and you will feel better about yourself while keeping things very happy on the home front. Compromising takes a little getting used to, but when you master this trait you will maintain harmony in your relationship. It will no longer cause you headaches at night and you will never be sleeping in the doghouse again.

Compromise is a difficult feat for many couples. Often, a woman will eat at a restaurant chosen by her husband, even if she prefers another place. But as a good husband and partner, you must ask your wife where she wants to eat and respect her choice.

Women love to try new restaurants that have just opened up or different types of food, not just steak and potatoes every time. Perhaps your wife may want to experience international foods. Ask her.

John: "As an example, Lisa wanted to try Vietnamese food for a unique change. I hadn't heard good things about that type of food but decided to give it a go. We went to the restaurant and ended up falling in love with the Vietnamese egg rolls."

Don't complain or nag all the way to the restaurant. Enjoy yourself and keep an open mind about different foods. After trying a new restaurant, if you or your wife don't like it, don't get mad at her or make her feel guilty. This will only make things worse. Treat this as a learning experience and don't go back to that particular restaurant again. At least you did your good deed for the day and made your wife happy by compromising and agreeing with her choice of restaurant.

Compromising is a powerful tool to keep your woman happy. You will see that she appreciates the things you do together much more. It's the little things that really mean a lot to her and they don't cost a penny.

Listen to her needs about what she likes and the hobbies she likes to do, then surprise her with those things when she least expects it. These are the little things that will keep her happy for many years. They're the things she will remember first when you are at fault and she will forgive you faster.

Her special needs might include an occasional back rub or just rubbing her feet after she gets home from work; or having a hot bath ready with her favorite book and letting her read alone for awhile.

Lisa: "One of the greatest things John does for me is just rubbing my feet after I get home from work. When he does that, even if it's just for a few minutes, it reminds me how much he cares for me and it makes me feel good about myself."

The little things you do will be remembered for a long time, such as unloading the dishwasher, making the bed for her, cooking once in awhile, doing laundry, washing her car, etc. Some of the little things that only take you a few minutes will create a big difference in your relationship.

Be considerate. At times, she may feel like staying home or may not want to go out with your friends because she had a rough day at work. Support her and don't nag her to death. Spend some quality time alone with her.

Lisa: "For example, one Saturday night a friend of John's was having a party and we had been planning for a couple of weeks to go to it. The night of the party I wasn't feeling too well and didn't feel like going anywhere. John really wanted to go to the party because the whole gang was going to be there; but he decided he would stay home and take care of me to help me get better. By John staying home that night, he showed me he really cares for me. Believe it or not, that was one of the most romantic nights we ever spent in front of the fire."

Show her tremendous love and let her know she is your best friend. Laughter is the best medicine. Make her laugh so she can forget a rough day. Give her some wine to relax and comfort her. Take the phone off the hook and devote all your attention to her. Put on some soft music, dim the lights and make her feel special. Make love to her for a long time. This will be one of the best nights of her life. She'll always remember these special nights when you made her feel like a queen.

In addition to compromising, keeping your wife happy, and making her feel like a queen, you need to spend quality time with your children. Read them a story every night for at least fifteen minutes. If you can help them with their homework they will really appreciate that.

If you have teenagers, talk to them about their problems in school and about their activities. Go to their sporting events and really involve yourself with their activities and extracurricular events.

Give them freedom to spend time with their friends but make sure they are aware of the things out there at that age, like sex, drugs and alcohol. Help to guide them in the right direction and listen to their feelings and needs. They want to be heard and they also like to participate in adult conversation. Develop well-planned events aimed at teens. Otherwise, they will express their dissatisfaction clearly and with great vigor.

It isn't always easy to spend seventy hours a week working and doing other household chores, fifteen hours with your wife communicating about important things, and spend time with your children. But being a good father is something that will make your wife love you forever. When a man spends quality time with his family doing different daily activities and sharing pleasant outings during the weekend, he can strengthen both his marriage and his ties with his children.

Mark and Angie have two girls. On the weekends Mark takes Angie and the girls to listen to him play in his band. This is a great way for family involvement and the girls love to listen to their dad play the drums.

If your children have grown up with such family time, it should be easy to get them to continue the same practice. Be a good family man and a good husband.

Chapter Three

TAKING TIME FOR INTIMACY

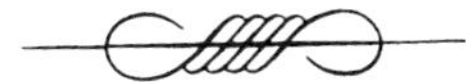

Love lasts as we draw breath. Aged love, like aged wine, becomes more satisfying, more refreshing, more valuable, more appreciated, more intoxicating.

—Madeline L'Engle

Creating time for intimacy is critical for maintaining the sweetness of your relationship. Take the time to hold hands, spend the day in bed, curl up on the couch, or take a romantic walk and watch a beautiful sunset.

Make yourself better than any other man. Make her feel better than any other woman. A woman will never quite know what it is that makes her so attractive. She could guess that it's her figure. But love is not born of breasts and bottoms alone. She may think it is her face or her great personality or wonderful sense of humor. You need to let her know what turns you on about her.

As we said in Chapter One, communication is vital to a good relationship. It is also the key to great lovemaking. Let her know your feelings about her. Making love should be fun and sporadic. Some evenings it may be long and romantic, but you can also have spur-of-the-moment quickies.

You may need to change your way of thinking. Make the occasion more romantic. You don't need to spend incredible amounts of money. It's the little things that we discussed earlier in this book that can make a difference.

To set the stage: a single rose, two candles by a bathtub full of bubbles, a chilled bottle of wine and two crystal wine glasses to help you relax. Take her in your arms and kiss her passionately, touching her very softly.

Be flexible and accommodate your partner. Be patient and considerate of your mate's feelings and body. Know what you enjoy and learn to ask for it. Talk about your feelings, needs and wants. Share your personal reactions but remember to be kind to each other.

When Bill and Michelle told us some of their intimate secrets, they shared with us some of the things they ask of each other so their lovemaking experience is more satisfying and more pleasurable. Bill asks Michelle what the most sensitive area of her body is and what she likes for him to do. He likes to accommodate and please her before he even gets a chance to enjoy himself in bed.

Michelle is very open with Bill when it comes to her body. She is very specific about what areas of her body are the most sensitive and most pleasurable, the areas that will help her climax sooner and with more strength. He makes sure she is completely satisfied and then he asks her for some of the things he needs to get aroused and to feel totally satisfied during lovemaking. Bill always waits for Michelle to reach orgasm before his own satisfaction. This example shows how considerate and accommodating he is during sex.

Enjoy your sexuality as part of a total relationship. Don't use sex to fix problems or to solve arguments. See sexual relating as a chance to enjoy equality of giving, receiving and sharing. Be playful and have fun.

Don't expect perfect performance every time. Be accepting of each other's tiredness or limits. Teach each other and learn from each other. Always make sure that sexual activities are combined with holding, hugging and snuggling. Tenderness is important. When your wife is tired, you don't have to make love for a long time. Even a few minutes of intimacy are better than not being together at all. Make love to her gently and passionately for a few minutes and then hold her and make her feel wanted and needed.

Lisa: "John knows that when I'm tired after working all day at the salon and preparing a healthy dinner, I don't always want to make love. Some lovemaking sessions may be short and sweet, and others may be long, tender and everlasting. Just make sure you have an understanding with each other. For example, some evenings when I'm tired from working all day, I may agree to make love to John only if it is a quickie. Other times on weekends when there is less stress, we may have gourmet lovemaking for a long time. John is a very considerate husband."

John: "I make sure that Lisa is satisfied before bed by giving her a nice back rub and lying next to her by the fireplace. Sometimes just cuddling together by the fire or in bed will make the night very special even if you don't have any kind of sexual activity. Even reading in bed can be a great way to be close and just be together."

Keep your eyes open for all possible places to make love when you go on weekend drives. If you discover a place you like, check it out. Bring a pillow and a blanket along with a picnic basket with your favorite wine or drink. The wonderful thing about making love outdoors is that it's romantic and erotic. You can make love almost anywhere.

If you only make love in bed in the evenings, your lover will expect this scenario every time you're going to make love. Therefore, it becomes routine. Use your imagination. Have you made love in the shower, the living room, the hallway, the backyard, in the hammock, etc.?

Show her how your mind works and how it revolves around sexual fantasies about her. Sexuality is a need, a drive. It can encourage us to ask for what we want, learn to give as well as receive, and affirm that we are whole and lovable just as we are. Because partners are vulnerable to each other, sex also requires trust. You show each other your bodies with their imperfections. You let go, release, make noise in very private ways.

Since each partner has different moods, rhythms, attitudes and values about sexuality, it is critical to discuss sexuality and sexual needs. Both partners can learn about their own sexuality as well as the sexuality of the other. A very important aspect of a healthy sexual relationship is respect and appreciation. Healthy sexuality is an attitude rather than an act. It involves sexual pleasure, but also a sexual connection.

Turn her on with the sensuality of your passionate lovemaking. Be her most passionate partner and greatest lover.

Chapter Four

Learn to Laugh and Play

I realize that humor isn't for everyone. It's only for people who want to have fun, enjoy life, and feel alive.

—Anne Wilson Schaef

Life can be difficult and serious. Newspapers and the daily news are filled with negative stories that can put a damper on your life. Life has it share of disappointments, illnesses and losses. We get so caught up in the things that are disappointing and negative in life that we forget to stop and smell the roses. We need to learn to laugh on a daily basis; learn how to dance, play and enjoy ourselves.

We need to be able to laugh at ourselves and at our mistakes. We need to realize that sometimes we do foolish things and we are not perfect. Take time with your wife to laugh and do fun things. Make life better for the both of you. Take time to feel joy.

A good marriage relationship can provide you with the security and comfort you might need to let your hair down. Let yourself loose and be silly and playful. Wrestle around with each other, but don't be too rough. For most couples, reading newspaper comics or a funny book helps them relax and forget about everything.

Lisa: "We love to sing to each other and change the words of a popular song, adding our nicknames to the lyrics. Also when a good song comes on, we like to dance around the house and laugh and enjoy each other's company."

John: "One of the funny things Lisa does is skip around the house and act like she is a little kid again. Also, she likes to talk in a funny kid language that makes me crack up every time. She comes up with funny nicknames for me and she changes them every couple of months. The latest name she has for me is Yood. Just to give you an idea of her little name calling, she used to call me Babe at the beginning of the relationship and then after three months it changed to Babers and many more after that. The one she had for me before she gave me Yood was Ludel. She got that name from yodeling one day. She is a lot of fun to be around. She's one of the best friends I've ever had."

Lisa: "John, on the other hand, likes to tell jokes all the time. He makes me laugh until my stomach hurts. He comes up with sayings that only stand-up comedians think about. He is so quick and witty. Some of the things he comes up with are crazy. John is my best friend in the whole wide world."

These are the things that will keep your marriage full of life and full of energy. Don't ever let your relationship get boring or lose touch with your friendship. Once you lose sight of each other, it is sometimes difficult to get it back.

Mark and Angie like to hop on their motorcycle and forget about everything that has happened during the week, including any personal problems they may have. They put on loud music and away they go for a long ride up to the mountains. They both have matching leather jackets and matching helmets. They are a cool couple. Mark also likes to crack jokes all the time. He is a very funny individual, which makes him a great friend and companion. This is what we call having a good time and feeling young again.

The most important part is to treat your wife like she is your best friend. Remember that you can have fun doing many activities and then come back to reality feeling better about yourself and about this crazy world we live in.

Another good stimulant that is fun, relaxing and helps you forget about reality, is video games. They help to temporarily release you from all your problems. At least once a month, we go to a video arcade and play with all the machines. A favorite is the air hockey machine because we can both play at the same time. We love to challenge each other! Whenever you play these games, let loose. Try it! It's great!

It is also helpful to find friends who love to do the same things you and your wife like to do. Go out to dinner and to the theater. Go to the movies and watch a comedy flick that makes no sense whatsoever, but makes you laugh. Those are the best movies. You forget about all the stresses of life and all the negativity that is around you day in and day out.

We love to get together with couples every weekend. We are all very compatible and we enjoy doing the same things together. It is important to be compatible with other couples, just because it gives you a chance to be with your friends and your wife with hers. You are all in the same place, but the women are talking about their women things and the men are talking macho about their favorite subjects like sex and sports.

We don't believe in *girl's night out* or *guy's night out*. Why should you do that when you can all be together? This is very healthy for the relationship because you get a break from the everyday monotony and have some space when you are with your friends.

Some people do things spontaneously. Others have to plan a day when they can relax, be playful, or be romantic. Make sure you leave at least one day out of the week to be together and do the things you would not normally do during the week. We usually spend twenty hours a week doing things that are fun or just joking and laughing and having a great day together.

Our favorite day is Sunday. We play, watch movies, eat junk food all day (this is the only day we do this), make love a couple of times and then watch some more movies. We love Sundays! That's our day to do whatever we want. We turn off the phones and pagers and we forget about the whole world.

A few couples told us that their schedules are too busy to spend fifteen or twenty hours a week doing fun activities. We can't stress enough how important it is to have a special day like our Sunday; a day without stress and without work.

Remember, the couple that plays together stays together

We have found this to be a very common saying for couples who have been together for a long time. They have shared this very important secret, so we hope many of you will take advantage of it and put it to use as soon as possible.

Another couple we interviewed, Julie and Ron, make a special date night. This is a night when Ron might pick Julie up from work and take her out to dinner and dancing. Other times, they will get a baby-sitter and stay home for a romantic bubble bath and massage night. Date night is very important to Julie and Ron.

Life is too short. Have fun now and you will live longer and be happier.

Chapter Five

Trust and Honesty Equals a Successful Relationship

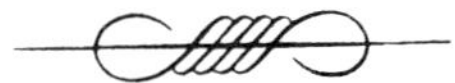

There is more hunger for love and appreciation

in this world than for bread.

—Mother Teresa

Trust and honesty are the bright, golden threads of any relationship. The husband must be honest and have an open communication with his wife. To feel secure, a wife must trust her husband to give her accurate information about his past, his present and his future. What has he done? What is he thinking or doing right now? What plans does he have? She needs to know if she can trust the signals he sends on a daily basis. She needs a foundation on which to build a solid relationship.

The wife who can't trust her husband to give her the information she needs also lacks the means of negotiating with him. Negotiation between a husband and a wife forms an essential building block to the success of any marriage or relationship. Without honesty, trust and openness a couple can resolve or decide very little.

Honesty is one of the most important qualities in a successful marriage. When you are married, you must send and receive accurate messages and responses. One or both spouses often make the major mistake of feeling one way and responding in another. When you fail to be honest about how you feel and where you are in that moment, your mate may wind up missing the target and both of you will end up frustrated.

Negotiation between a husband and a wife forms an essential building block to the success of the marriage. Many married couples often use the expressions, "Where are you at this moment?" and "What can I do to make it better?" to find out how the other one feels. If you project that you are feeling a particular way, your spouse will respond with an appropriate action or accommodation.

If your wife asks you to go out to dinner and you feel like staying home and having a sandwich, then say so. Don't just agree with her every time. Be honest and tell her how you feel at that particular moment. Compromising is important, but make sure that it is a fifty-fifty deal.

Voice your opinion to your wife when you are really tired and you want to sit by the TV and have some quiet time at home; but promise to take her out to a nice restaurant the following night. This way you can be honest with her and make her happy by pleasing her at a later time. She will appreciate this more than you know. It's better this way than to go out to dinner in a bad mood and spoil the entire evening. Once again, honesty is one of the most important qualities in a successful marriage.

What happens when a marriage lacks honesty and openness, leading to the ultimate dishonesty of an affair? Can coming clean with your spouse help or does it spell sure death for the relationship?

Be honest at all times

Honesty is the best marriage insurance policy

We should emphasize that a woman needs to trust her husband. Whatever advantage a man may gain in being secretive, closed, or even dishonest, he wins it only at the expense of his wife's security and marital fulfillment. She must find him predictable. A blending of minds should exist so that she can read his mind. When a woman reaches that level of trust, she is able to love more fully.

When the wife hears the truth from her husband (about what he thinks, what he plans to do with his life, where he has gone and where he wants to go), she can respond to him with security and confidence. She knows she can influence him, urge him to take her interests into account, and affect his decisions. When a husband honestly communicates with his wife, it allows her to contemplate the future more accurately and to plan accordingly — two very important factors for most women.

Love, honor and cherish one another.

Love your wife as you love yourself.

Love your wife as your own flesh.

Ephesians 5:21

Chapter Six

Having a Positive Marriage

Love never dies of natural death. It dies from neglect and abandonment. It dies of blindness and indifferences and of being taken for granted. Things omitted are often more deadly than errors committed.

—W. Somerset Maugham

This chapter addresses passion and your state of mind; how being positive and optimistic every single day can make your life and your marriage brighter and full of energy. Having a positive outlook in life will make you a star, whereas a negative attitude can make you a loser.

You can create miracles for you and your loved one. That is the power of positive thinking. Change your belief system and focus on the positive in life. People who continuously focus on the bad things put themselves in a state that supports those types of behaviors. Have you ever noticed that people are drawn to positive people? On the other hand, negativity will push them away.

You must first take a good look at yourself. You have to be honest and think how you act in front of others everyday. Do you act cheerful from the time you wake in the morning until you go back to bed at night? Ask yourself the following questions:

- How do I come across when I talk to people?
- Do they see me as a positive or negative person?
- Do I sound optimistic and passionate about life?
- Could I have more energy if I change my beliefs?
- How can I make my wife love me more?

If you answered honestly and need some pointers, we will give you a few. We are confident they will help you be more passionate about life and help your relationship in the process.

Passion is one of the secrets that has kept many successful people and many marriages going for years. It is the one attribute that gives the energy and the obsessive power to achieve and to grow. This passion will strengthen your relationships. It has the power to help you love more and it will provide the energy to do more things with your wife and kids.

Being passionate will make you stay up late and get up early in the morning. It gives your life the power and energy that will spread to your family and friends. Many relationships and marriages will survive because of the power of passion. Even when things go wrong, you are still smiling and you make everything look better and more attractive in life. If you are passionate about life, you will give your wife a better life with fewer worries.

What about beliefs? Beliefs are the compass and maps that guide us toward our goals and dreams. They give us assurance that we'll get there. Without beliefs or the ability to tap into them, people can be totally helpless and without the power to change their lives. They're like a speedboat without a motor or a prop. With strong guiding beliefs, you will have the power to take action and create the world you want to live in. Beliefs help you recognize what you want and energize you to reach fulfillment and to make your wife, family, and friends very happy for many years to come.

To change our own behaviors, we have to start with our convictions. If we want to model excellence, we need to learn to model the ideology and behaviors of those who achieve excellence and happiness. The birth of excellence and happiness begins with our awareness that our beliefs are a choice. You can choose those that either limit you or support you. The trick is to choose the beliefs that are conducive to success (which will bring you the results you want) and to discard the ones that hold you back.

In all of our interviews, the subject of being negative and always thinking the worst about everything was one of the biggest complaints we came across. The wives said whenever their husbands were in a bad mood or depressed, they would begin to feel the same way, even though they may have had a good day themselves.

John: "When Lisa has had a bad day at work and she comes home in a bad mood, I try not to get caught up in the negative waves. I talk to her and let her vent so she can get all the anger out. Then, I try to make her feel better about her day by giving her positive feedback and perhaps a nice neck rub to release the stress and tension. After fifteen minutes of listening and being considerate of each other's feelings, we are ready to have a nice evening with positive thoughts. By doing positive things, we enable the next day go smoother."

Don't ever let negativity ruin a perfectly beautiful day if your partner is in a bad mood or if she has had a bad day. Take fifteen minutes of your time and be considerate with your wife. Sympathize with the way she feels and make it all better. Be positive at all times. It will make the world look brighter and it will make her appreciate you more.

If you learn nothing else from this book, please review all that we teach in this chapter. The power of a positive state of mind and positive thinking are important to happily succeed in your personal and professional life. Take a good look at yourself and change the way you think and act. This will change your life forever.

Chapter Seven

Imagination Goes a Long Way

Love one another, but make no bound of love; let it rather be a moving sea between the shores of your souls. Fill each other's cup, but drink not from one cup. Give one another of your bread, but eat not from the same loaf. Sing and dance together and be joyous, but let each one of you be alone.

—Kahlil Gibran

A little imagination can go a long way when it comes to pleasing your wife sexually. What would it take to make your sexual life more exciting? What improvements can you make without thinking too much or spending a lot of money?

We are not talking about going out and buying expensive sex toys or those weird lotions that are on the market these days. It is not about buying costumes to pretend you are someone else. It's all about doing little things during the day when you are together around the house; little things that are going to make a big difference in your life.

Give lots of kisses

Experimenting with different kinds of kissing can improve your sexual life tremendously and can turn your woman on a lot faster. Use your tongue and explore your wife's lips, then pull her into a slow and sensual kiss. When you do this, you and your wife should feel like you are in another world and you will kiss a lot longer than usual. The end result is a slower buildup to a larger explosion for both.

Take a bath together

After the kids are in bed, for those of you who have kids, take a bubble bath together. Dim the lights and get a couple of scented candles of your choice, put on some romantic music or sing to your wife if you know how to sing, get crazy in the tub and enjoy her company. Turn the phone off or take it off the hook and forget about everything except your wife. Give her all your attention and pamper her. Rub her feet, neck, shoulders, and other private parts. Show her how romantic you can be.

Tell her how beautiful she is and how good she looks with no clothes on. Women love to hear that often. They feel good about themselves and it builds their confidence levels. Pull out the rubber ducks your kids play with in the tub and have fun with them. If you have some adult toys, take them out also and play for a long time. Bath time has never been so much fun.

Shower together

When you take a shower together, treat her like a queen. Wash her hair and make sure you get deep into her scalp. Women love that. There seems to be a little sensitive spot up there that turns them on. After you are finished with her hair, wash her back with lots of soap and a big sponge, then move down to her buttocks and caress them for awhile. Kiss her a lot in the shower and make it nice for her.

Make sure that the kids are out of the house so she can relax and enjoy her shower with you. I know that Lisa can't relax unless she knows that absolutely everyone is out of the house and nobody is coming over any time soon. Do the same when you are planning to have a romantic shower. Turn all the phones and pagers off and have a wonderful time.

If you shower at night, you should also use candles to make the ambiance more romantic. Make love to her in the shower sometimes. Changing where you make love once in awhile makes it more exiting.

Creative lovemaking

Be creative in your lovemaking. The oral sex position is good when you concentrate on each other more. Doing the old 69 is okay but you do not concentrate on your partner as much as when you do it individually.

Try to make your wife your main focus. Some men forget about their partner's feelings and what she likes or dislikes. Keep lovemaking simple and try to wait for her to climax first. This is a big problem for most women. In our interviews, many women told us that they enjoy making love with their husbands but they wish that it could last longer and that their husbands would wait to climax until they were fully satisfied.

Many men have a problem with premature ejaculation. In most cases, they come to a climax soon after they begin intercourse. This usually happens within the first thirty seconds of intercourse and women don't even get a chance to become aroused. Sad but true, thirty seconds is the length of an average television commercial.

The result is that men climax quickly for their own release, leaving their wives aroused but unfulfilled. The secret to this problem is making sure your wife has an orgasm first by having a lot of foreplay and by making sure she is totally aroused before you have intercourse. There are many adult toys out there that can help your wife have an orgasm before having intercourse and that will make her satisfied every time you make love.

Also, let her show you the things that she does and the places she touches when she is alone. Ask her specific questions about her private places where she gets aroused the fastest.

This has helped Mark and Diana tremendously. At the beginning, Mark had a problem with this. He did not wait for Diana to orgasm, but after she opened up and told him what she needed, their lovemaking is perfect every time. This problem only lasted for two months after they started making love, because Diana was smart enough to communicate with Mark about her needs.

Please make sure that you work in this area and ask your wife what she needs from you during sex. Make her happy every time by making sure she is satisfied in bed before you climax.

Eat junk once in awhile

Being on a diet or just eating healthy all the time is okay. However, once in awhile it is good to eat some of those great tasting fatty foods like candy bars, cakes, ice cream, hot fudge, etc. Eat them together. Take the food to bed.

Feed each other and make a buffet on her tummy. Put all the food on her, lick it and get silly.

This will lead to other fun things. For some reason, when you eat junk food you feel more playful, perhaps because of the sugar rush you get when you eat all that stuff. You are probably thinking that eating in bed is too messy. So what if you have to sleep on a few crumbs or on a sticky spot?

One of the movies that seems to be popular with the couples we interviewed was *9 1/2 Weeks*, where Mickey Rourke is feeding Kim Basinger different kinds of food in bed. It may sound messy but in that movie the scene was very sexy. If you've never seen this movie, rent it and enjoy the scene; and if you are adventurous enough, try this at home with your wife.

Buy her sexy lingerie

Buy her some sexy lingerie and make her feel like one of those models in the lingerie catalog. Tell her how sexy she looks and take some pictures. She is going to love you for that and in return you will get very spoiled in bed. She will show you how much she appreciates that kind of attention.

Light the way

One single candle lit during lovemaking can really put the passion in your marriage. In addition to the romantic lighting, the candle also serves the purpose of letting each other know that you are in the mood — without having to say a word.

Mark the calendar

The week following her period she gets more into sex. Her libido is on low boil and she will climax a lot faster and more intensely. Many women also enjoy making love when they are on their period. For some reason their sex drive increases during that week and they like to be pampered during that heavy hormonal week. If you can handle a little mess, try to make love during that time of the month.

Talk to her in bed during sex

Tell her how good she feels and ask what she wants you to do to her. You can learn a lot from her by talking during sex. Moan, scream, and talk dirty! This really works in all marriages and relationships. Don't be embarrassed. Make her feel like a wild woman.

Women love to hear sexy things while making love. They like it when their husbands tell them what they are going to do to them and how. For some reason this type of approach turns them on more and they seem to orgasm faster. Talk to your wife in bed while making love, but make sure that she doesn't get offended with some of the things that you tell her, because when you are in the middle of having sex and you're talking dirty, things come out that may be inappropriate and she may take it the wrong way.

Never give up on pleasure

The big orgasm! If your wife does not have an orgasm during intercourse, don't give up. Try everything in your power until she does. Toys are good, different positions and more foreplay. Ask her where she wants to be touched and what she likes. She is the only one who knows what turns her on.

There is no reason why any woman today should put up with less than satisfying sex from her husband. You should always make sure to take the initiative to give your woman an orgasm every time. She may not want one every time, but it is much appreciated if you try every time.

What happens if you find that your wife is unable to have an orgasm? If, no matter how hard you try, she still can't have an orgasm? This is a very common female sex problem. There are usually two principal reasons for it, both of which are easily remedied.

First, she may not be relaxed enough. She might be thinking about household chores or work-related issues. She may be trying too hard to have an orgasm. She must relax and let it happen by itself.

Second, your lover may need more caressing and more stimulation in the areas she knows will turn her on, or you may be ejaculating too quickly.

To solve the first problem, you might have a glass of wine to relax her and then try to lie in bed and not think about anything but the two of you. Let all the other worries disappear. Make the moment special with some soft music and turn the lights down. Give her a little massage. Massage can be very arousing. Read a good book or a magazine that will help her get turned on. Tell her not to worry about reaching an orgasm and not to feel any pressure. Have her join you in having sex and forget about the orgasm until it creeps up on her. It will happen.

The second problem is a little tricky. Your lover might not be totally turned on by the time you are ready to have intercourse. Make sure you tease her for awhile and increase foreplay. Women don't like it when men jump into bed and want to have intercourse right away. Caress her gently; touch her breast and kiss her passionately. Ask her if she is ready to have intercourse. Talk to her. Ask her questions that are going to help you bring her to an orgasm. Satisfy her every time.

Read together

Read romantic, sexy novels or the hot letters in a pornographic magazine. Your wife will get so turned on by the time you are done reading. Try it! This has worked wonders for many sexual relationships.

Bill and Michelle were having a problem with intimacy for awhile when it came to sex. They were not enjoying their lovemaking sessions like they did in the beginning of the relationship. They were bored with the same routine and the same positions they always did. They needed a change in their sexual relationship and lovemaking experiences.

They decided to subscribe to a couple of pornographic magazines to see what other couples were doing to make their sex more satisfying. Now they both enjoy lying in bed and reading the hot, nasty letters published every month in this magazine. This sexually arouses them. After they read the letters, they like to browse through the magazine and look at all the pictures of beautiful women and hot looking males to get more turned on. Sometimes they like to try some of the positions shown in the magazines.

Bill and Michelle said that since they started doing this, their sexual relations are more intense and more enjoyable. They recommend that all couples subscribe to a magazine or buy a romance novel that will help get them in the mood and enhance a great lovemaking experience every time.

Be adventurous and try new things to spice up your love life and your relationship.

Take the initiative

The best thing you can do is to be an instigator sometimes. When she is working on the computer, come up behind her and start kissing her neck, ears, and elsewhere. If that doesn't work, you can always whisper in her ear how much you want her and what you are going to do to her. More than likely, she'll get off the computer and come straight to bed. This will bring wonderful lovemaking.

Another one of our couples shared with us that when they go to a party, they like to play little games on each other. Sometimes just to excite him and turn him on, she goes to the party without any panties on. Then when he's talking to some other woman, or he's right in the middle of a serious conversation with some friends of his, she makes sure no one is looking her way except him, then she lifts up her dress so her love toy is exposed. He can never resist it and he gets really turned on. At the end of the evening he takes her home and he usually has his pants open before they arrive. They have intense sex the moment the front door is closed, with her dress around her hips and her shoes still on.

This couple has shared with us that their favorite tactic is tempting each other sexually in places where they find it difficult to do anything about it. The more public or offbeat the location, the more likely they are to get aroused.

Make love often

We have come to realize that quantity is important. It's easier for her to get turned on if you have sex more often. The more you do it, the more your wife will shower you with affection and the happier you will be. We know you are tired after work, but put in the extra effort. Drink a cup of coffee, take a caffeine pill, do whatever you have to do to become more energized. Show her how much of a stud you are and take her to bed at least four nights a week. You're the man!

Let her be in control

Being in control is very important for your wife once in awhile. Women love to feel dominant in bed. Be sexually aggressive and adventurous. Let your wife call the shots one of these nights when you are making love. Make her feel like she is the boss. Let her tell you what she likes best. Learn from her fantasies and desires.

Don't hold back. What do we mean by that? Here's an example of this kind of situation. Mike and Sheryl are a very close married couple. They have been married for twenty-one years. After all this time together they are still crazy when it comes to having sex. Mike lets Sheryl be sexually aggressive and adventurous in bed. He lets her take charge and decide what they are going to do sexually. Once in awhile he acts like he is her slave and he does anything she asks for. This is one of their favorite things to do.

At the beginning it was hard for Mike to do this. He felt threatened when she wanted to try new things. He accused her of wanting to dominate him. Sheryl explained that she didn't want to dominate him, she just didn't want to hold back.

After awhile, Mike started to let Sheryl do what she wanted. He didn't feel very comfortable at first, but eventually he let her do several things that changed their lives. He started by letting her hold him without a lot of genital rubbing. Then he let her perform oral sex on him in different positions and with different kinds of foods and flavors. Mike never thought that oral sex could be better than regular sex. That was the first time that he was able to ejaculate during oral sex.

Since that experience, Mike and Sheryl play these great games in bed. Mike is happy that he tried something new and that he let his wife be in control that evening.

Have fun in bed and let her show you some new things during sex.

Chapter Eight

CONTROLLING THE CONFLICTS

When you have nothing left but love, then for the first time you become aware that love is enough.

—Anonymous

No relationship or marriage is without conflict. We all have differences of opinion, preferences, ideas, and even direction. You need to express your feelings and ideas even if it causes some stress or arguments in the relationship. A relationship is only as strong as the conflict it can survive. What we mean by this is that the relationship will show vitality and strength based on the way the conflict is resolved. Once all differences are resolved, the relationship can move to a different level of power.

Many of us are scared of conflict or arguments because we don't know how to fight. We are afraid we may lose our cool and say things we don't mean. We may even be afraid we'll become vicious, violent, or even physically destructive.

Some of us cannot control our anger as well as others. We may be afraid the other person will start yelling and throw or slam things which will trigger the inner animal in us that is uncontrollable. This kind of behavior can be very dangerous to many people who have been abused in the past. But even these people can learn to express anger in a constructive way.

When you have a fight and resolve it in an adult manner, both of you will feel you have discovered something that helps you know one another better.

Here are some helpful hints on how to control your fights and arguments with your loved one:

1. Try to pinpoint why you are mad or frustrated. Try to be specific so the argument has some foundation and you don't fight over something stupid.

2. State your feelings and why you feel that way; how it made you feel when she did the thing she did.
3. Tell her what you need to hear from her--an apology or a good excuse.
4. After the apology has been given and accepted, ask one another if the conflict has been resolved.
5. The most important hint is this one: kiss, hold one another, and make up.

Also, when having these fights, concentrate only on the present problem. Don't bring up things from the past that have bothered you or that you have been holding inside. We are only human and we all make mistakes that help us grow and learn about life.

One more thing that we learned from others is that when the fight is getting out of control and things are being said that you don't mean, it is better to leave the room or the premises until you cool off. Never, and I mean never throw things at each other or raise a hand to each other. It does not resolve anything, it just makes things worse. Leave the house, the party, the park, etc. Do not lose your cool.

When you think you can talk in an adult and rational manner, come back and finish the argument. If you do or say something wrong, you can never take it back from her memory and it will affect the way she thinks of you. After the little fight or argument, love her more; love her always.

Hugh and Michelle said that it is only natural for a healthy relationship to have little fights and misunderstandings. The little conflicts they have had have made their relationship a lot stronger. They have learned what the other one likes and dislikes, and what each of them needs from the relationship.

They shared with us that when they have arguments about anything they are not happy with, they sit down and talk it out. They never hold anything inside; they like to get everything out in the open. Then when the same situation comes up again, they don't explode at each other and cause a bigger argument or fight.

At the beginning of their relationship, Hugh and Michelle had a big fight that turned really ugly. They could not come to an understanding of the problem and Michelle moved out of Hugh's house. They were only apart for a short period of time and later got back together. They learned a lot from this experience.

They agreed that from that point forward, they would resolve all the conflicts and disagreements as soon as they happen. They will resolve them in a rational manner without moving out of the house and without being violent. Michelle said in our interview that since that incident three and a half years ago, they have not had a fight. They have resolved all their differences by talking to each other and by compromising.

Be kind to one another,

tenderhearted, forgiving one another,

as God in Christ has forgiven you.

Ephesians 4:32

Chapter Nine

The Importantance of Physical Attraction

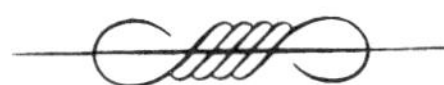

Every single ancient wisdom and religion will tell you the same thing - don't live entirely for yourself, live for other people. Don't get stuck inside your ego, because it will become a prison in no time flat.

—Barbara Ward

Looking good for your wife is very important for the survival of your relationship. Many men do not take care of their bodies after they get married. Women want to be proud of their husbands in public. They want to feel important when they walk into a party holding hands with a good looking man.

We don't mean that the husband has to look like a swimming suit model, a stripper or a movie star. By calling for you to be attractive we mean you should take good care of yourself to look something like the man your wife married, keeping the qualities she saw in you when you first met. After all, that was the man she fell in love with, not a movie star or some other fantasy.

Hugh and Michelle made a promise to each other that they would keep in good physical shape by eating healthy foods and by working out together on a regular basis. They are really dedicated to each other when it comes to nutrition and working out. They enjoy doing this together and they support each other while doing it.

Every morning they get up and have wheat English muffins with egg whites and fat free cheese, along with a protein drink. Then they go to the basement of their home where they have a full-size workout room and they work out together until they have done their training routine. They make it really enjoyable by listening to their favorite music while working out.

Hugh and Michelle urge husbands to try to do this with their wives and to be consistent. It feels good to be in good physical shape together.

Many men lack the will power to get off the couch and go for a bike ride or just go for a walk.

Being a couch potato is very common in this country. We tend to work all day, come home, have dinner and a couple of beers or some wine, and then forget about everything else. This is not the ideal man.

Those of you who have found the woman of your dreams think you don't have to look good anymore because you don't have to impress anybody else. You are married and don't want to be noticed anymore, possibly to avoid temptation from other women. But what you fail to realize is that even though you are married, you need to keep up your physical appearance: clean shaven, teeth brushed, deodorant, nice cologne, and a nice haircut.

Many women complain about how much their husbands have changed since they met them. Each remembers how good their man used to look; how physically fit he was, how neat he kept his home or apartment, and how his personal hygiene really impressed them.

After the big day (the wedding) a lot of that good stuff went away. The husband has now gained forty or fifty pounds, he forgets to shower and to brush his teeth in the morning, does not use deodorant or cologne, and his feet stink. What happened to that cool, tidy, fit and good-smelling individual? He is gone and too often he is gone forever. Many men think that because their wives love them unconditionally, what they look like doesn't matter. Nothing could be further from the truth.

Often, visual stimulation arouses a woman sexually. If you look good, she will look at you often and like what she sees. If you look bad and don't take care of your personal hygiene, she won't like what she sees. She will be turned off and in some cases, even repulsed.

When a woman looks at her husband and is disappointed by what she sees, it puts her in a terrible bind. First, she starts thinking that the physical attraction she once felt for him has probably gone forever. Second, she tends to notice other men, especially nice looking men, which makes her feel guilty. She may not wander into an affair, but she remains vulnerable nonetheless.

You can guard against these dangers by making a reasonable effort to stay attractive and well groomed. One simple test of your attractiveness is how much your wife wants to fondle you. The visual stimulation she receives by looking at her attractive husband will arouse her sexually. Most husbands don't mind it very much because they recognize it as an indication that their wives find them physically attractive.

In another test of your attractiveness, you should ask yourself what your wife says about you in public. Does she give compliments or does she put you down? Women often express their enthusiasm about their husbands in public with their friends. They like to show off a good-looking man. When a woman says too little about her husband, she may not see much reason to talk about him. Listen to what your wife says when you go to a party or to a friend's house and learn from it. Make her happy and give her the man she once knew and married.

A woman also wants an attractive husband as a pure and simple matter of pride. People often see a woman's ability for success in terms of her husband's appearance. When a woman has an attractive husband, it says she has the appeal and the talent to deserve someone of his caliber. When a woman's husband lets himself become unattractive, the message comes across loud and clear that she couldn't get someone better and she may even deserve him. She has little to offer, the world decides, and she attracts little in return.

Today's market has an abundance of books, videos, programs, and a multitude of other products designed to help men and women shape up, dress with style, color your hair properly, and many more things. Do some research and keep looking good for your wife.

Don't let yourself go! Your wife really wants to keep the man she married. It is said that looks aren't everything, but it is important to keep the relationship alive. This is the reason why many women have affairs--because they want to be turned on again by a good-looking guy who is full of energy, is outgoing, and has the motivation and will power to look and smell good. So let all the women look at your nice body and fantasize about you. You don't have to have any temptations; you love your wife and that is all that matters.

We have discovered that husbands who are fit and have good personal hygiene tend to have sex more frequently than those who do not care about their personal appearance. Women get turned on with sexy cologne, a nice pair of briefs, or sexy G-string underwear.

Be her exotic dancer for life. Dance for her in the bedroom and show her what you've got. We know that it is difficult to get motivated to go for a walk after dinner or to go to the gym, but many people have done it and you can too!

One of the secrets we have learned from many married couples is that if you and your wife do all these things together as a team, you can achieve the way you want to look and spend quality time doing the things you want to do.

Try to cook together as a couple. Make healthy meals together, eat fewer sugars, more vegetables, no potato chips (only on Sundays), and drink more water. The secret is in the way you eat. Remember that you are what you eat. If you eat badly you will look bad, and if you eat good you will look good. When you go out to dinner, stay off the butter and the fried foods. Eat things from the menu that are not fattening and you will look and feel a lot better.

Try this for awhile and you will see how your energy level and your sex drive begins to increase. You will be having sex more than ever before or just as much as when you first met her. She will be proud to show you off in public and will want to spend more time with you!

Chapter Ten

Having Time and Space for Yourself

The life and love we create is

the life and love we live.

—Mother Teresa

Having time alone for a couple of hours to enjoy whatever activities you want to do is not only extremely important, it's a necessity. It will enable you to build a stronger relationship between you and your wife. This time alone can give you a chance to think, pray, and get in touch with your inner feelings to figure out what you want out of life. When you have your space to do the things you enjoy the most, it creates a sense of understanding about being in a relationship and being alone.

Everyone is different. Some people like to go fishing and others just like to sit in front of the TV and watch their favorite show or sport. Whatever it is you love, make sure you do it at least once a week. This enables you to get away from reality and to decrease the stress you experience day in and day out.

This time apart from your spouse will give her a chance to do the things she loves the most, like shopping, reading a book, or taking a hot bubble bath. It will enhance your marriage tremendously. Both of you will be more relaxed and you will want to spend more time together, which is very important in a relationship.

If you have kids, take them to the grandparents and pick them up in the morning. This will give you the opportunity to have some peace and quiet, get your thoughts together, and forget about everything; not to mention lowering your stress levels.

Try to do things or go places where you can find peace and renewal. After your little getaway, you will find yourself more refreshed and energized, and more efficient in doing your daily tasks.

Tell your wife what you've learned and what you've gained during your time alone and she will feel very special when you share this wonderful experience of peace and serenity.

Alan and Monique love to get away every couple of weeks by themselves and forget about everything. What they like to do is pack their backpacks with food, a bottle of wine, and a few blankets, then hit the road.

They like to get in the car and head up to the mountains and try to find secluded areas where not too many people visit. A major part of the fun is the adventure together of searching for a welcoming, secluded road that invites them to see what beautiful areas are kept secret. The more secluded the better. They pick some of the highest areas in Colorado where they can see all the beauties of nature.

They like to hike up trails and find the most sensuous spot with a view that becomes very special to the both of them. With such a beautiful view, they can't help feeling in a loving mood; watching the clouds slip by, having the high grass swaying all around them in the breeze and the warm sun's rays dappling their bodies between pine boughs.

After they find an area they like, they put the blankets on the ground, take the wine out of the basket, and begin their relaxing day. Then they proceed to talk about positive and delightful things that make them feel good which gets them in the mood to make love and to cuddle up together. Alan and Monique get closer to each other every time they get away and spend some quality time together.

Part of the beauty of these adventures is that you can take the whole day to find them and you can always return to your favorite spots in the future. Driving along a country road, an especially secluded Aspen grove may call to you. It's just a simple matter of keeping your eyes open for them. They're there; you only have to notice their presence and accept their invitation.

Alan and Monique have been doing this little ritual for twenty-two years, and it doesn't get old. They used to live in Hawaii for many years and they enjoyed the same intimate aloha adventures there. Getting away and finding a peaceful place without people, phones, pagers or traffic is one of the ways they get back their serenity and get in touch with each other again.

Chapter Eleven

Interviews and Highlights

Love is a direct gift from God, the most powerful and potent life enhancing human energy, and possibly life's only meaning.

—Mother Teresa

We interviewed many married couples in preparation for this book. All of the interviews were very good and very informative, and they made a lot of sense. The ones we are going to mention in this chapter are the ones that impressed us the most.

Mark and Angie Wilson

We've known the Wilson's for awhile and we admire them very much because they have the whole package; they have it all figured out. The Wilson family consists of Mark and Angie, and their two daughters, Mandy and Heather. They are each very special in their own way.

Mark is a supervisor for the CBI (Colorado Bureau of Investigation) and has worked there for about twenty-five years. He is very good at what he does. His favorite things to do are sports and his motorcycle.

Angie runs a child care business out of their home. She is very good with children and also very educated. She teaches the children how to be polite and about everyday things they will need in the future. Her favorite things to do are gardening and riding on the motorcycle.

Mark is a very aggressive individual who likes to have a lot of toys. What do I mean by aggressive? Well, he likes to work hard and he knows what he wants out of life. When he sets a goal, he achieves it. He wants the best for his family and is always thinking of them first. Mark works hard and plays hard, but his main attractions in life are his wife and his toys.

Angie, on the other hand, is very humble. She doesn't ask for much. She is an understanding and giving wife. She is very smart when it comes to managing money. She also loves kids and she loves her family very much.

Mandy and Heather are the best behaving teenagers we have ever met. They help around the house. They both like to work and are very responsible. They are two kids any parent would be proud of.

What are the things that impressed us about this family? Well, the whole package. So we wanted to find out how they do it and then share it with you.

Mark and Angie have been together for twenty-seven years and they are still so much in love with each other. We asked them about what they thought was the secret of their successful marriage. Mark answered, "Space." Anytime he needs some space to get away from everything and everyone (his creation, as he puts it) he always gets it. Angie gives him the space he needs and he is happy with that.

In the beginning he wanted to be alone watching his sports or going for a bike ride by himself to forget about everything. Now he says that having space is being with his wife; jumping on the motorcycle and going for a long ride, letting all the worries fade away, or going out of town to see a football game, forgetting all the stresses of life and forgetting about reality for awhile. Having space is the thing that has worked for them all these years to get rid of stress.

Another secret they shared with us is that they know when an argument is not worth fighting.

They think about it before they say anything that might hurt the relationship. This is a good point!

They told us they have not had a fight for a long time. In fact, they do not remember the last time they had a fight and that's because they know to stop and think before they say or do something in haste.

Their communication is very well rounded. We asked Mark how his communication with his wife was. His answer was short and sweet, and Angie agreed. Mark said that there is nothing that happens to him or to them that Angie does not know. He tells her everything he does and everything he is planning to do. She is always a part of his decisions and his life.

Mark and Angie have nights when they spend quality time together. They know that these nights have helped them tremendously. Mark sends the kids out of the house and the two of them go out for a nice dinner. Then they come home and make love and enjoy each other.

One of those nights when they were alone, they didn't time it right and the oldest daughter came home and caught them in the middle of the act. Angie was really embarrassed at the time, but she talked to her daughter and everything was fine. Angie and her two daughters have a very open relationship with open lines of communication.

It is impressive that after twenty-seven years they act like newlyweds in bed. This is a lesson all of us should try to learn. Make a point to spend quality time together with your spouse to make love or just hold each other for awhile in front of a fire with a glass of wine. This can keep the spark in your marriage alive forever!

Last but not least, they do a lot things with their kids. They go to all of the kids' functions, games and activities. Spending quality time as a family is also very important to a healthy marriage. If the kids don't give you a hard time, things stay more peaceful in the relationship--less problems to resolve and fewer arguments.

As we said before, the Wilson family is a very impressive family we could all take lessons from.

Judeh and Diana Comandari

Another couple we are really close with is our brother and his wife, Judeh and Diana Comandari. Judeh and Diana are parents to Robert, Alex, and Stephanie. They have been together for twenty-eight years.

One of the things that impress us the most is that they compromise a lot. They have learned that the power of compromising is wonderful in their relationship. They asked to share a story:

Judeh was born and raised Catholic. He did not believe in any other religion and that was that. Diana was also born and raised Catholic, but after a few years of being married she decided to change religions without discussing it with her husband. She became a Jehovah's Witness and she also changed all of the kids to that religion. They stopped going to church as a family and problems developed. They argued all the time about different beliefs and different customs. It wasn't good.

Judeh decided he would give his family the freedom to choose whatever religion they wanted to follow and he would try to understand their reasons. He learned to compromise and to sacrifice.

This is one of the biggest gestures anyone could do to keep peace and to keep the family together.

They are very happy now and he is learning a little more about the religious beliefs of his family. Believe it or not, this compromise not only kept the family together, it brought them a lot closer.

Mike and Rita Salazar

The Salazar family is another one that really impresses us. Mike and Rita have been married for forty-two years and are very happy together. They are both retired now and they love to do things together everyday. They are each other's best friend and are the perfect couple because they love and respect each other so much.

What we admire most about this couple is how close they are with each other, their kids, and grandkids. They have raised all of their children to be very loving and very respectful. The Salazars have good family values. One of their sons, Tony, is an honest and loving individual who is the image of his parents when it comes to caring for others and helping family stay together.

Mike and Rita have taught their children the same family values they have followed all of their lives. This is one of the things that has helped them stay together for forty-two years. When asked the secret of their successful marriage, they replied, "Honesty."

Honesty is one of the most important qualities in a successful marriage and they are true believers of this. They always tell each other how they feel and what they want. The feelings they express to each other include good and bad feelings, their frustrations, problems and fears; anything that is on their minds. They say they learned that from the Bible and it is called "two becoming one."

In the beginning of their relationship it wasn't easy for them to open up and it was even harder for Mike to express his feelings. But after a few years of practice it became easier to cope and to express all their feelings to each other.

Their suggestion is that you, as a husband, be honest from the beginning. Don't hide anything from your wife because eventually she will find out. Tell her the truth about any problems that you may have. Remember that when you said I do, you became a team--you became one. You can fix and beat any problem that may come up if you attack it with the power of love and togetherness.

Doug and Marla Smith

Doug and Marla have been together for twenty-two years. They shared with us many positive things about their marriage.

Doug is a pharmacist at a hospital. His passion always has been pharmaceuticals and the practice of medicine. He is a very hard working individual, sometimes working sixty hours a week. He loves to give Marla all the good things in life. His favorite pass times are hiking and making love to his wife in secluded areas.

Marla is an interior designer. Her favorite hobbies are hiking in the mountains and beautiful music. She has a passion for the beautiful things that nature has to offer.

Doug and Marla live in a beautiful home on top of a mountain in Evergreen, Colorado. We asked them what was their secret to a successful marriage. They shared with us that communication keeps them together. They talk for hours some days and they make sure everything that happens during the day is communicated to the other.

They do not watch television until they talk for at least an hour each day. Doug knows that Marla needs conversation to satisfy her needs. She would rather talk about her day and people she encountered than go to a movie or out for a fancy dinner. Marla said that she loves the verbal attention, but what she loves even more is giving the same attention to her husband. She enjoys some conversations in which the man talks only about himself and what he has done.

Chapter Twelve

Doing the Right Things will Make You Perfect in her Eyes

There can be no more fulfilling goal in

life than to love and be loved.

—Bob Conklin

This chapter will show you how to keep that magical spark in your relationship. These helpful hints will make all the difference in how your lover feels about you and will only take a few minutes of your time.

Go for a walk
and hold her hand.

Send her flowers
on an ordinary day.

See a movie of her choice
even if you don't want to see it.

Start a fire in the fireplace
on a cold winter night.

Make Mother's Day
a special day for her.

Shower her with kisses.

Open doors for her.

Always be a gentleman.

Watch a sunset
together in silence.

Leave her little love
notes on her pillow.

Buy her a single rose
and leave it in a conspicuous place
where she's sure to find it.

Give her a good foot or back rub,
or both.

Take a shower or a candle-lit
bubble bath together.

Surprise her
with a candle-lit dinner,
soft music, and a bottle of wine.

Let her have the remote
control once in awhile.

Wash her car for
no special occasion.

Go for a walk in the woods together.

Admire beautiful sunsets together.

Go grocery shopping together.

Playfully wrestle around
every once in awhile.

❖

Buy her a favorite CD and have it in the stereo
set at an appropriate song.

❖

Give her privacy to read
her favorite book.

❖

Buy her a day at the spa.

❖

Surprise her with tickets
to her favorite musical.

❖

Appreciate the small things
she does for you,
and don't take the big things for granted.

Spend a lot of time together
doing activities you both love.

❖

Go away with her
without the children
at least once a year.

Send her a card at work
just to say hello.

Clean up after yourself every morning.

Don't leave the house in a mess for her.

Ask her if she needs anything
when you go to the store.

Buy her favorite candy
and keep it hidden from the children.

On cold winter mornings,
heat up her car
and scrape her windshield.

Prepare her favorite coffee or tea
before she goes to work.

Surprise her with a new outfit
or lingerie every once in awhile.

Take long walks and
pick her a flower.

When you enter a party
hold her hand and
let everyone know she's with you.
Be proud.
She's your queen.

❖

Help her decorate the house;
after all, she needs your input too.

❖

Take care of her when she's sick.

Replace the toilet paper when it runs out.

Always put the toilet seat
down after you're done.

When you go to the bathroom
in the middle of the night,
try not to wake her.

Laugh a lot together.
It will get you through tough times.

Do the laundry for her,
but don't mix colors
or use too much soap.

Unload the dishwasher for her.

Call her in the middle of the day
just to say you love her.

Make her comfortable in every way you can.

Fluff her pillow or get her a blanket.

❖

Just hold her in your arms.

Buy her some romantic bubble bath.

Stop and ask for directions when you're lost.

Be polite.

Ask her to slow dance
when you go out.

Read her favorite poetry.

If you forgot her birthday, have a good excuse.
If you forgot your anniversary,
move out of town.

Chapter Thirteen

Saying the Right Things will Put a Smile on Her Face

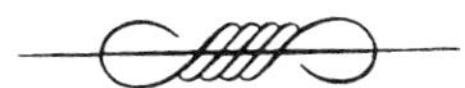

A life lived in love

will never be dull.

—L.F.B.

Not only your actions but what you say can have a big impact on your relationship. We are often preoccupied with our daytime jobs or evening chores and many times we forget to say those special things that our special someone likes to hear. Here are some helpful hints on what to say to enhance your relationship:

In the morning when you first wake up
say, "Good morning" and "I love you" to start a good day.
This endears you to your lover
because she knows you are paying attention.

❖

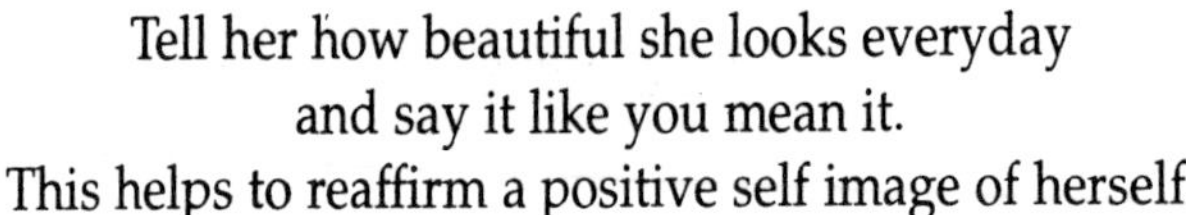

Tell her how beautiful she looks everyday
and say it like you mean it.
This helps to reaffirm a positive self image of herself.

Call her by her pet name frequently.

Tell her to have a wonderful day.
This will make her feel good.

Flirt with her once in awhile.

Call her during the day
to tell her how much you love and miss her.

Tell her how you want to take her
on a romantic weekend getaway,
just the two of you.

Tell her some good jokes
at the end of the day
and make her laugh a lot.

Never swear at her.

Tell her how smart and clever she is
and how proud you are of her
and her accomplishments.

Ask for her advice
on any problem that you may have.

❖

When you're wrong, admit it.

❖

Talk to her when you are worried about money.

❖

Always be polite.

❖

If you want to know what she likes
and what she feels,
listen to her carefully and she will open up.

❖

Show her respect.
If you abuse your wife
verbally or physically
you will have no relationship.

Remember, no one ever wins a fight.
Do you want to be happy
or do you want to be right?

Arguments always have three sides:
his, hers, and the facts.

When she goes away on a trip,
let her know how much you missed her.

When she is talking,
let her finish without interrupting.

Never be rude to your wife.

Three kind words can warm her soul.
"I Love You"

If you don't feel like doing something,
tell her why.

❖

Talk to her calmly.

Give her praise often.
She can live for a long time
on a good compliment.

Be honest,
but don't tell her things
that might hurt her feelings.

Tell her she is sexy.

Don't hesitate to say you are sorry.

Tell her that she turns you on--
visually, emotionally
and sexually.

Pray together at night.

Tell her she is the object of your desire.

Chapter Fourteen

The Romantic Touch (Quotations of Love)

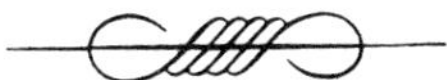

Be glad of life because it gives you the chance

to love, work, play and to look up at the stars.

—Henry Van Dyke

Many famous people all around the world have made the following quotations throughout the ages. They are sentiments of the affection they felt for their loved ones. Read them. They will fill you with happiness and love.

This is my pledge, dearest one, I will stand by you...
And no matter whether the wine be bitter or sweet
we share it together and find happiness in the comradeship.

Edith Bolling Galt (1872—1961)

My little one [his wife], one understands oneself, I imagine.
You will never know exactly how and how much I love you;
nobody knows it except me.
But you almost know. I miss you enormously.

Arnold Bennett (1867—1931)

Never did I believe there could be such utter happiness in the world,
such a feeling of unity between two mortal beings.
I love you. Those three words have my life in them.

Alexandra (1872—1918)

Afterward we will be as one animal of the forest
and be so close that neither one can tell
that one of us is one and not the other.
Can you not feel my heart be your heart?
Ernest Hemingway (1899—1961)

❖

All that you are,
All that I owe to you,
Justifies my love, and nothing,
Not even you,
Would keep me from adoring you.
Marquis de Lafayette (1757—1834)

❖

Little Heart you don't know how much feeling I have for you.
You are like my child, and my greatest friend, all in one!
I don't believe there has been a woman in Ireland
Loved the way I love you for a thousand years.
John Millington Synge (1871—1909)

Ask the child why it is born;
Ask the flower why it blossoms,
Ask the sun why it shines.
I love you because I must love you!
George Upton (1834—1919)

A good leg will fail, a straight back will stoop;
A black beard will turn white, a curled pate will grow bald;
A fair face will wither, a full eye will wax hollow.
But a good heart, my love, is the sun and not the moon.
For it shines bright and never changes, but keeps its course truly.
If you would have such a one, take me;
And take me, take a soldier; take a king.
William Shakespeare (1564—1616)

But if it pleases you to do the duty of a true, loyal mistress and friend,
and to give yourself body and heart to me, who have been and will be,
your very loyal servant (if your rigour does not forbid me)
I promise you that not only the name will be due to you,
But also to take you as my sole mistress,
Casting off all others than yourself
Out of mind and affection, and to serve you only.

Henry VIII (1491—1547)

❖

But my heart beats through my entire body
And is conscious only of you.
I belong to you;
There is really no other way of expressing it,
And that is not strong enough.

Franz Kafka (1883—1924)

I fell in love with her courage,
Her sincerity,
And her flaming self-respect
And it's these things I'd believe in even
if the world indulged in wild suspicions
that she wasn't all she should be...
I love her and that's the beginning of everything.
F. Scott Fitzgerald (1896—1940)

To love and to cherish.
It was always music in my ears,
Both before and after our marriage,
When my husband told me that I was the only one
He had ever thought of
Or cared for.
Mary Todd Lincoln (1818—1882)

Sensual pleasure passes and vanishes in the twinkling of an eye,
But the friendship between us, the mutual confidence,
the delights of the heart, the enchantment of the soul;
These things do not perish and can never be destroyed.
I shall love you until I die!
Voltaire (1694—1778)

I love you soulfully and bodyfully,
Properly and improperly,
Every way that a woman can be loved.
George Bernard Shaw (1856—1950)

A few days ago I thought I loved you;
But since I last saw you I feel I love you
A thousands times more.
All the time I have known you
I adore you more each day;
That just shows how wrong was La Bruyere's maxim
That love comes all at once.
Everything in nature has its own life
And different stages of growth.
I beg you, let me see some of your faults:
Be less beautiful, less kind, less good...

Napoleon Bonaparte (1769—1821)

Your letter has been a balm to me. Be happy:
be as happy as you deserve to be:
it is my whole heart that speaks.
You have given me my share, too,
of happiness, and a share very keenly felt:
nothing else can have for me
the value of a token of remembrance.
Napoleon Bonaparte (1769—1821)

I miss you even more than I could have believed:
and I was prepared to miss a good deal.
So this letter is just really a squeal of pain.
It is incredible how essential to me you have become.
I suppose you are accustomed to people saying these things.
Damn you, spoilt creature;
I shan't make you love me any more
by giving myself away like this — But oh my dear,
I can't be clever and stand-offish with you:
I love you too much for that.

Vita Sackville-West (1892—1962)

There is only one situation I can think of
in which men and women make an effort
to read better than they usually do.
When they are in love and reading a love letter,
they read for all they are worth.
They read every word three ways;
they read between the lines
and in the margins....Then,
if never before or after they read.

Mortimer J. Adler (b.1902)

❖

I did not know I loved you
till I heard myself telling you
so — for one instant I thought
"Good God, what have I said?"
and then I knew it was the truth.

Bertrand Russell (1872—1970)

Love looks not with the eyes,
But with the mind;
And therefore is winged Cupid
Painted blind.

William Shakespeare (1564—1616)

The hours I spend with you
I look upon as a sort of perfumed garden,
a dim twilight, a fountain singing to it...you
and you alone, make me feel that I am alive....Other men
it is said have seen the angels,
but I have seen thee and thou art enough.

George Moore (1852—1933)

Your words are my food,
your breath my wine.
You are everything to me.
Sarah Bernhardt (1844—1923)

There's only one thing
greater than my fear — that is my love.
My love will always conquer my fear — but
it can't do it immediately.
It needs the full force of my love to do it
and it takes days for that to emerge
out of its dark hiding places.
John Middleton Murry (1889—1956)

I have loved you for three years
with my heart and my mind,
but it seems to me I have never loved you
avec mon ame, as I do now.
I love you with all our future life-our life together
which it seems only now to have taken root
and to be alive and growing up in the sun.... I have never
felt anything like it before.
In fact I did not comprehend
the possibility of such a thing.

Katherine Mansfield (1888—1923)

I love thee with a love
I seemed to lose
with my lost saints.
I love thee with the breath,
smiles, tears, of all my life!
And if God choose,
I shall but love thee better
after death.

Elizabeth Barrett Browning (1806—1861)

Those who love deeply
never grow old;
They may die of old age,
But they die young.
Sir Arthur Wing Pinero (1855—1934)

Conclusion

Congratulations! You have read all the chapters and hopefully have practiced some of the things in this book. By now you are on your way to being a better husband, a better friend, and a better lover in your marriage.

All the information, secrets, and suggestions in this book are here for you to read over and over again until they become natural to you, making your wife very happy and more in love with you than ever.

Continue to keep the lines of communication open. Don't hide anything from your wife. Tell her often how you feel about her. Share with her your innermost passions and all the things you want out of life.

Communication is the key. No matter what is going on in your life, it will get better if you communicate with your loved one. By talking often you will find out that you can fix any problem that may arise and if you put your heads together, everything will work out.

Don't forget to work hard and play hard. Laugh together, dance, sing, and joke around as much as you can. Pray and stay healthy together. Love one another as much as you can and never take anything for granted.

Be active and be silent. Express your feelings as often as possible and make love to your wife frequently. Celebrate who you are as individuals and who you are as a couple.

We learned this from a very wise uncle in Central America, Uncle Jorge Zedan. We will never forget what he said to us one day, "Your marriage is like a plant. Couples are either growing or dying. Don't let the plant die. Water the plant often, take care of it, and once it has grown, spread it around. Give some of it away to others. Take the seeds out of it, spread them, and then water them some more. Don't let the plant die. If you do, your marriage and your love will be gone forever."

Share this book with others and help them be better husbands. Show them how to treat their wives with more respect and how to appreciate them more. Show them what you've learned from this book and tell them how it has improved your marriage.

We sincerely hope this book will change your life forever by opening your heart and your wife's heart to love more and to understand each other better.

In the pages of this book we have expressed the love, the ideas, and the experiences of others to help all married couples stay together forever. This is a great joy for us and we hope we can touch your hearts in the future.

Best wishes,
John and Lisa Comandari

Appendix 1
The Domestic Checklist

Often times women with full-time jobs work harder at home than men. Wives are doing about 33% more chores than the average husbands are. It is only fair for husbands to do their equal share of chores in the household. Over 72% of married women help bring home the bacon so it's time for men to help with at least 50% of the chores.

Most likely the checklist we have prepared for you will show some discrepancies and the list for the women is going to be longer than the men's list. If this is the case for you, it has to change if you want to keep your wife happy. Unfortunately this is normal in almost every marriage.

Some household solutions:

We received many tips from our interviewed couples and one thing most agreed on is to utilize professional services to accomplish some of the chores. For example, you might hire a cleaning service to come in every couple of weeks to help with the detail cleaning you don't have time to do on a daily basis. You might also hire a landscaping company or even the neighborhood kids to mow the yard, pull weeds, and do the gardening. Another example of saving time is to take the clothes to the dry cleaner so your wife doesn't have to iron all your clothes.

Many wives complain that one of the things they dislike is coming home after a long, stressful day at work and having to cook a meal for her husband and family. To help the situation you might do take-out dinners or maybe order pizza. Another simple solution would be for the husband to prepare the evening meal one or two nights a week. If you don't know how to cook, you can buy a cookbook or ask your wife how to make certain foods. Even if you make soup and sandwiches you will make your wife extremely happy because she will have more time to spend with you and the kids. A little effort is all it takes.

Dividing the household chores equally is going to take some effort. Forget gender roles as a basis for division. Use common sense and courtesy. Who gets up last in the morning? That person should make the bed. Whoever is home first in the evening should start preparing dinner.

Another helpful hint is for the last one who leaves in the morning to throw in a load of laundry and the first one to come home in the evening can transfer it to the dryer. Somehow chores that are done together seem less of a burden than those done alone. The idea here is not to divide the list by a rigid formula, but for each of you to pitch in to establish a routine in your weekly schedules. In this way the repetitive chores can be taken care of during the week so that you, your wife and family can have your weekends free to have fun doing various activities together.

The Domestic Checklist:

Make sure you divide household chores equally to accommodate one another and to make your day-to-day lives easier. The checklist below can be fun and can help you become more productive. Put a check mark by each chore you and your wife are agreeing to do and stick with it; but keep in mind that you may trade different chores at any time so they don't get monotonous.

Chores	Husband	Wife
Make the bed	________	________
Make coffee	________	________
Cook breakfast	________	________
Feed the kids	________	________
Feed the pets	________	________
Make lunches	________	________
Buy groceries	________	________
Mow the lawn	________	________
Mop the floors	________	________
Vacuum	________	________
Water the plants	________	________
Do the laundry	________	________

Chores	Husband	Wife
Drop off dry cleaning	________	________
Iron	________	________
Wash windows	________	________
Clean out garage	________	________
Barbecue outside	________	________
Pay the bills	________	________
Do the taxes	________	________
Fix the car	________	________
Clean the toilet(s)	________	________
Paint the house	________	________
Shampoo the carpets	________	________
Repair the faucet	________	________

Chores	Husband	Wife
Make dinner reservations	________	________
Take the kids to school	________	________
Take the pets to the vet	________	________
Buy gifts	________	________
Send out holiday cards	________	________
Call the baby-sitter	________	________
Change diapers	________	________
Buy wine/liquor	________	________
Set the dinner table	________	________
Go to the bank	________	________
Schedule appointments	________	________
Fix the computer	________	________

Chores	Husband	Wife
Plan the vacation	________	________
Help the kids with homework	________	________
Do activities with the kids	________	________
Go clothes shopping	________	________
Attend parent/teacher conference	________	________
Take the kids to the doctor	________	________
Plan for college	________	________

Other chores in your household:

____________________	________	________
____________________	________	________
____________________	________	________
____________________	________	________

Now go back through the list to make sure it's not lopsided with one person doing more than the other. If the list is not equally divided, use a colored marker and mark each chore to indicate who should be doing it, not who does it now.

Always look for ways to make your chores seem easier. For instance, you might use a duster on the furniture instead of using a cloth with polish every single time. Another tip would be to keep your home free of clutter by picking up after yourselves at the end of the day. Your home will always appear cleaner than it is. In other words, cleaning as you go is the answer to a cleaner, more organized home.

Appendix 2
Tell Me the Truth

We have designed a questionnaire for you and your spouse to find out which areas you need to focus on. We have made two identical sections, one for the husband and one for the wife.

In order to improve your relationship with your spouse, please answer these questions honestly. Review them often to insure peace and happiness in your marriage.

After completing the questionnaire, spend some time with your spouse going over it and comparing yours with hers/his. Decide which areas you can work on together and which will need work from you alone.

Today is the day to start planning for the future. Don't wait until tomorrow to improve your marriage.

Husband

First, rate the following marital needs on a scale from 1 to 10, with 1 being most important and 10 being least important at this time. Be honest.

After you do this, try to focus on each of them and ask yourself how you and your spouse are going to achieve better results in those areas.

____ Communication

____ Compromising

____ Honesty and openness

____ Sexual relations

____ Physical attraction

____ Other: ______________________________

____ Affection

____ Recreational companionship

____ Space (time for yourself)

____ Having a positive outlook

____ Admiration

____ Other: ______________________________

Answer the following questions honestly by circling the appropriate answer or filling in the blanks:

1. How would you rate your communication with your spouse?

   Great Good Fair Poor

2. Do you spend quality time with your spouse talking about daily events and future goals?

   Always Frequently Sometimes Seldom Never

3. How often would you like your spouse to talk to you? (hours per day) ________________

4. What would you like to talk about the most? ________________________________

   ____

5. Do you talk to your spouse with loving words?

Always Frequently Sometimes Seldom Never

6. Do you tell your spouse how much you love her?

Always Frequently Sometimes Seldom Never

7. How well do you listen to your spouse?

Always Frequently Sometimes Seldom Never

8. Do you show you care about her needs?

Always Frequently Sometimes Seldom Never

9. Do you recognize when you are wrong?

Always Frequently Sometimes Seldom Never

10. Do you admit when you're wrong and say you're sorry?

Always Frequently Sometimes Seldom Never

11. Do you feel more comfortable talking to someone else other than your spouse?

Always Frequently Sometimes Seldom Never

12. If you do feel more comfortable talking to someone else, explain why.

____

____

13. How are you at compromising?

Great Good Fair Poor

14. Do you do activities your spouse likes to do, without complaining?

Always Frequently Sometimes Seldom Never

15. Do you compromise by giving up some of the things you like to do to meet the needs of your spouse?

Always Frequently Sometimes Seldom Never

16. How many times per week are you intimate with your spouse? _________

Is this frequency enough for her? Yes No

Is this frequency enough for you? Yes No

17. How often would you like your spouse to engage in sexual activities with you?

(times per week) _________

18. Do you make love to your spouse in special places? (other than the bed)

Always Frequently Sometimes Seldom Never

19. Do you make time to have fun with your spouse; for instance, a date night?

Always Frequently Sometimes Seldom Never

20. Do you spend quality time doing things that you both like?

Always Frequently Sometimes Seldom Never

21. Are you honest and open with your spouse?

Always Frequently Sometimes Seldom Never

22. Do you feel honesty will improve your marriage? Yes No

23. What is usually the major cause of conflicts between your spouse and you?

____

____

24. How might you avoid future conflicts? ______________________

____

25. How are you at dealing with conflicts?

Great Good Fair Poor

26. How important is physical attraction to you?

Extremely Somewhat Not much Not at all

27. Do you make an effort to keep in good physical shape?

Always Frequently Sometimes Seldom Never

28. Do you do things together as a couple to keep in shape?

Always Frequently Sometimes Seldom Never

29. What are some things you could do to get in shape together? ____________________

____

30. Do you feel you would have more energy to make love to your spouse if you were in better shape? Yes No

31. Briefly share how an attractive spouse could satisfy your marriage? ________________

____

____

32. Do you have quiet time alone, without your spouse, to do things you like to do?

Always Frequently Sometimes Seldom Never

33. What do you find enjoyable doing alone? ______________________________

____

34. As a couple, do you get away from your normal routine for fun?

Always Frequently Sometimes Seldom Never

35. Would you like to get away (just the two of you) more often? Yes No

36. Where would you like to go or what would you like to do? ______________________

____

37. What are some of your individual goals for the next five years? ____________________

____

____

38. What are some of your goals as a couple for the next five years? ____________________

____

____

39. Are you happy with the way things are going in your marriage at the present time?

Yes No

40. If you are not happy with your marriage right now, what specific things might you do to improve the relationship? ____

41. What specific things would you like your spouse to do to improve your relationship?

42. What do you want out of life? ______________________________

____

43. Do you feel you are a positive person?

Always Frequently Sometimes Seldom Never

If you circled *sometimes*, *seldom*, or *never*, how can you change your actions or way of thinking to be more positive? ______________________________

____

____

44. What are some things you might do to make your home life more fulfilling?

____

____

____

45. List the things you are going to change about yourself — starting today:

____

____

____

Wife

First, rate the following marital needs on a scale from 1 to 10, with 1 being most important and 10 being least important at this time. Be honest.

After you do this, try to focus on each of them and ask yourself how you and your spouse are going to achieve better results in those areas.

____ Communication

____ Compromising

____ Honesty and openness

____ Sexual relations

____ Physical attraction

____ Other: ______________________________

____ Affection

____ Recreational companionship

____ Space (time for yourself)

____ Having a positive outlook

____ Admiration

____ Other: ______________________________

Answer the following questions honestly by circling the appropriate answer or filling in the blanks:

1. How would you rate your communication with your spouse?

   Great Good Fair Poor

2. Do you spend quality time with your spouse talking about daily events and future goals?

   Always Frequently Sometimes Seldom Never

3. How often would you like your spouse to talk to you? (hours per day) ________________

4. What would you like to talk about the most? ________________________________

   ____

5. Do you talk to your spouse with loving words?

Always Frequently Sometimes Seldom Never

6. Do you tell your spouse how much you love him?

Always Frequently Sometimes Seldom Never

7. How well do you listen to your spouse?

Always Frequently Sometimes Seldom Never

8. Do you show you care about his needs?

Always Frequently Sometimes Seldom Never

9. Do you recognize when you are wrong?

Always Frequently Sometimes Seldom Never

10. Do you admit when you're wrong and say you're sorry?

Always Frequently Sometimes Seldom Never

11. Do you feel more comfortable talking to someone else other than your spouse?

Always Frequently Sometimes Seldom Never

12. If you do feel more comfortable talking to someone else, explain why.

____

____

13. How are you at compromising?

Great Good Fair Poor

14. Do you do activities your spouse likes to do, without complaining?

Always Frequently Sometimes Seldom Never

15. Do you compromise by giving up some of the things you like to do to meet the needs of your spouse?

Always Frequently Sometimes Seldom Never

16. How many times per week are you intimate with your spouse? __________

Is this frequency enough for him? Yes No

Is this frequency enough for you? Yes No

17. How often would you like your spouse to engage in sexual activities with you?

(times per week) _________

18. Do you make love to your spouse in special places? (other than the bed)

Always Frequently Sometimes Seldom Never

19. Do you make time to have fun with your spouse; for instance, a date night?

Always Frequently Sometimes Seldom Never

20. Do you spend quality time doing things that you both like?

Always Frequently Sometimes Seldom Never

21. Are you honest and open with your spouse?

Always　　Frequently　　Sometimes　　Seldom　　Never

22. Do you feel honesty will improve your marriage?　Yes　No

23. What is usually the major cause of conflicts between your spouse and you?

____

____

24. How might you avoid future conflicts? ______________________

____

25. How are you at dealing with conflicts?

Great Good Fair Poor

26. How important is physical attraction to you?

Extremely Somewhat Not much Not at all

27. Do you make an effort to keep in good physical shape?

Always Frequently Sometimes Seldom Never

28. Do you do things together as a couple to keep in shape?

Always Frequently Sometimes Seldom Never

29. What are some things you could do to get in shape together? ____________________

____

30. Do you feel you would have more energy to make love to your spouse if you were in better shape? Yes No

31. Briefly share how an attractive spouse could satisfy your marriage? ____________________

____

____

32. Do you have quiet time alone, without your spouse, to do things you like to do?

Always Frequently Sometimes Seldom Never

33. What do you find enjoyable doing alone? ______________________________

____

34. As a couple, do you get away from your normal routine for fun?

Always Frequently Sometimes Seldom Never

35. Would you like to get away (just the two of you) more often? Yes No

36. Where would you like to go or what would you like to do? ______________________

____

37. What are some of your individual goals for the next five years? ____________

____

____

38. What are some of your goals as a couple for the next five years? ____________

____

____

39. Are you happy with the way things are going in your marriage at the present time? Yes No

40. If you are not happy with your marriage right now, what specific things might you do to improve the relationship?

___

41. What specific things would you like your spouse to do to improve your relationship?

___

___

___

42. What do you want out of life? ______________________________

____

43. Do you feel you are a positive person?

Always Frequently Sometimes Seldom Never

If you circled *sometimes*, *seldom*, or *never*, how can you change your actions or thinking to be more positive?

____

____

____

44. What are some things you might do to make your home life more fulfilling?

45. List the things you are going to change about yourself — starting today:

Summary